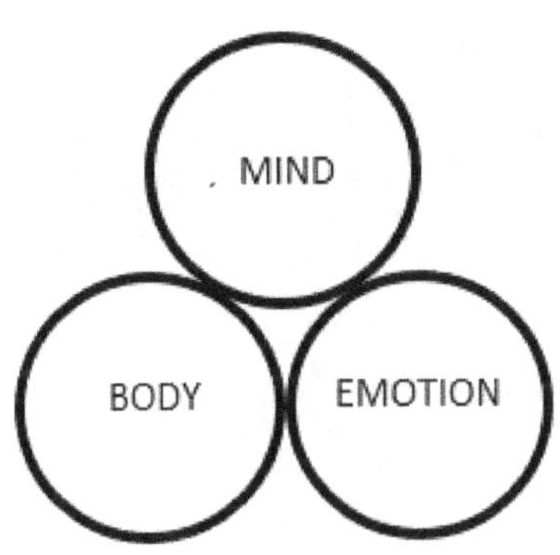

Mind, Body & Emotions I

Powers, skills, and functions for every human to master

Judy Moore

DEDICATION

To all my children and young adults everywhere.
May you know your powers and take them to new heights.

CONTENTS

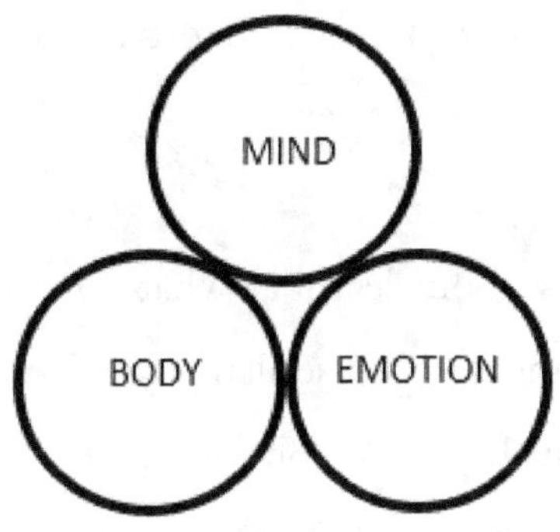

CHAPTER 1

POWERS

This book is about learning to develop yourself. You've already learned a lot about how to get along in this world, but there are likely many things you are unsure about or don't understand. Many people feel lost, powerless, or unhappy even through adulthood. General education provides a format for learning traditional subjects and is focused on memorization and competition. It does not teach self-development, nor how to relate to others or Self in a positive manner. People with advantages and support are in a better position to succeed and the rest must figure it out alone.

This book is about learning what your faculties and abilities are and how to use all that you have as a human being effectively so that you can achieve whatever you set out to accomplish. It identifies seven powers, three tools, fifteen functions, and five main skills you absolutely already have just from being human.

"Faculties" are defined as inherent powers. "Inherent" means a characteristic or feature that is an essential part of someone or something. Thus, powers are features we have the moment we come into this world. These powers must be shaped and expanded even if they are limited or constricted by experiences in childhood. They are always within you available for use. The sooner you learn to take charge, the easier it will be to navigate through your life with intention, purpose, and joy. Embrace and own them now with a willingness to learn how to use them wisely and effectively.

The Power of Awareness

Awareness is a key power because there is often a lot going on at one time. When you are not aware of what is going on around you or within, you miss important information and are more likely to jump to conclusions that aren't accurate. Awareness is important for safety in general so you can prevent or avoid negative experiences including accidents.

Awareness is a state of being where you pay attention to many things at once while also focusing on what you are doing. It is like tracking through observing. Imagine your body is a vehicle and you are using your tools, functions, and powers to navigate through intricate experiences. To increase awareness, you will want to slow down and take in a broad view. Observe, notice, look around, scan, feel, listen, continually to take in information.

Much like playing a video game, practicing awareness allows you to choose how to respond to surprises or look ahead at options - to see obstacles you may want to avoid or points of interest to explore. You have amazing senses, and you want to get as much information from the world around you and from signals within you as you can before making your next choice.

The Power of Choice

You need to use your power of awareness to give you information about what choices are available. You are learning to use your great tools of body, mind, and emotions to determine which choice you want to make every moment of every day. Understand and know that choice is a power you always possess.

Direct your choice of thoughts, feelings, and behaviors intentionally moment to moment. If you just respond to things around you, it can feel like you are tossed among the waves. Instead, choose what to do with your body – whether to get up and walk across the room or wash your hands. Choose what to think – whether to contemplate the universe as you look at the stars or consider what happened at the store. Choose what to feel – whether to put on comfortable or fancy clothes or stay frustrated at spilling a drink. It's the little choices we make every moment of every day that determine the bigger experiences – from having a great day to accomplishing a goal.

You have the power of choice in every moment, and if you make a choice that did not turn out well, caused harm or mishap, you will want to learn from that experience. It is normal to make mistakes and fail, but the better you get at identifying which choice will bring the outcome you seek, the more you will have successful experiences and prevent having to start over. Mistakes can be painful and embarrassing. They don't mean you are stupid or bad, but they do signal us to give more thought to different options before making a choice. The power of choice, like all our powers, must be developed.

The Power of Focus

Focus is the power you have to direct your energy into something specific whether it is a small object, a memory, getting on a subway or listening to a song. The power of focus allows us to explore the rich and varied details of experiences. For instance, we state that something is beautiful because we have tuned-in to the visual details that make it pleasing to the eyes and produce fascination. Something feels good physically or emotionally only because we hold our focus on the details that make it good and allow ourselves to sit in the experience of them.

To use the power of focus effectively, we must learn to hold focus for long periods of time and learn to move our focus around quickly. You absolutely have the power of focus, but you must work with it continuously to get better at operating it. When you are learning anything, you need to repeatedly focus on the details until they are committed to memory.

When your focus is split, and it feels uncomfortable or overwhelming, you likely need to snap your focus onto only one thing and take care of it. Sometimes, however, you may prefer to focus on several different things at once or move your focus back, forth, and around in brief intervals. Depending on what you are trying to accomplish, you will want to adapt your focusing style.

Focus is a way to take in information but also influence the world around us. If I am fully focused on what I am saying, I can better get a point across. If I am fully focused on what I am doing, I will pay more attention to details that enhance the outcome. If I am fully focused on feeling good, others will be more relaxed around me. Always choose what you focus on, practice to increase your ability to hold focus, and learn to determine how much is needed for each situation.

The Power of Habit

We are creatures of habit. Habits allow us to operate in automatic mode with some tasks so we can focus on others. The process of learning itself is one of developing a new habit. Habits are things we have done over and over again so that we now "know" them and don't have to think about them. We have habits of thoughts, habits of feelings and habits of behavior.

The power to create a habit can be used to make life easier, but habits will need to be updated from time to time in order to grow and develop. We come into this world with the power of habit, so we start making them immediately though we don't realize we are. So often we make habits early on that may have helped us in some way at the time but are definitely not helping us as we get older and have more experiences.

Any habit can be changed or updated in 30 days no matter how long we've been using it. In order to change a habit, we must use our powers of awareness, focus, and choice to catch Self in the habit, then stop and replace it with a new habit. This must be done all day throughout each of the 30 days as best you can until the habit is fully replaced. It can take less or more than 30 days depending on the level of focus. When you learn how to use this power and have successfully changed a habit, the process gets easier from there. You will realize that change is often necessary and good. You will also see that it feels much better to choose to change a habit rather than avoid or distract and feel pressure from outside forces.

The Power of Values

Every person has the power of values from the moment they come into this world. Values are things that are important to you. They can also be identified as strengths, talents, needs, weaknesses, or natural gifts. Values are things that you do a lot, can't seem to stop yourself from doing, or that just seem natural or easy to you.

To the untrained eye, a strength or value can sometimes be annoying to others when we haven't learned to develop and use it effectively. You have many values with varying degrees of importance to you and this too may shift over time. The key is to make a list of things that are important to you or that you are struggling with and begin to engage in one daily with the purpose to develop it.

If you find that people get annoyed consistently with something you are doing, understand that this experience is signaling something important. It means that there is a valuable aspect, quality, or skill within that you have *not* recognized and need to learn how to use effectively to produce positive outcomes. Begin to listen to their negative feedback to determine what adjustments to make. Do not conclude that there is something wrong with you. Instead, look for what the situation is showing is needed and important.

Humans have a tendency to not see or ignore value in things or others or attribute value to things that are destructive or not necessary. The power of values is often not well or clearly developed and has led to devaluing. People often feel pressured to do things they don't value so not a lot of time is put into discovering what is important to the individual or what strengths and natural gifts they possess.

Sometimes it can be hard to see our values, but they are within all of us. It may be that you must choose your values. Since people are often not good at recognizing value, you don't want to wait around for others to point yours out. We do see some people have discovered talents early on and have been supported in developing them further. So, we often fall into concluding that we don't have value, or that we have to compete and put others down.

These experiences get us off track of determining and

developing our own power of values. Our values define who we are and the direction in life we want to go. Start by picking one thing that is important to you, of interest, a strength, or a weakness. Then, engage in it in some way for at least one hour every day. If you follow through on that daily commitment, you will develop and expand your power.

The Power of Balance

The power of balance is the ability to stay centered between two poles, opposites or extremes and includes physical, mental, and emotional balance. There are many polarities that exist in life including hot/cold, night/day, good/bad, happy/sad, etc. Polarities create movement in life. Think about how weather is created by the movement of hot and cold air masses.

Physical balance is tied to our center of gravity. It's that place just above the belly button where gravity pulls down and allows you to learn to stand and walk on two legs. Emotional and mental balance are maintained within your neutral center where you can sit in stillness, quiet, and peace. If you are always moving around, thinking about things, or seeking attention, it is difficult to find your power of balance. When experiencing emotional, mental, and physical extremes, there is danger of losing balance and therefore control over choices.

The goal is to use your power of balance to develop a strong center within your being. This will enable you to stay well-grounded amidst the ebb and flow, the ups and downs, the highs and lows of life. Recognize that these movements enable changes and growth to occur and with the power of balance you can dive, flow, rise above, or ground yourself on purpose and with greater success.

The Power of Healing

We all know we have the power to heal. We have all observed on several occasions how the body heals itself when the skin is broken or damaged. This is an amazing power we possess. The body always automatically begins to heal itself when functioning is disrupted. Study on how cells create new tissue and discard toxic wastes can be helpful to bring conscious awareness to and validation of this power. Deeper reflection and focused intention during the experience can further help one realize this force of power within.

Health is our natural state of well-being that is recognized by effective functioning, balance, positive experiences, and performance. Healing is the process we go through when effective functioning is being restored. The body, mind, and emotions are intricate networks of pathways that connect a vast variety of structures and elements. Restoration could include rebuilding of physical tissues which transport and use nutrients or reconnection of nerve fibers that transmit electrical charges. All pathways between structures need to be open for full healing to occur, so this is also an important part of the process.

We can enhance and accelerate the healing process by providing consistent attention through protection, understanding, clearing, and nurturing what has been damaged or imbalanced. This is true for the mind and emotions as well and not only because the nervous system is connected to emotional and mental signals moving through pathways in the brain. Deeply reflect to gain understanding into all the interconnections related to an experience.

The healing process takes time and is an experience of opening and awareness on many different levels - from the microcosmic to the macrocosmic. Restoration to well-being is the goal and part of the healing process is learning to replace choices that caused the damage or imbalance with choices that create wellness. Be fully present and engaged in your healing process and follow it through to completion. Use the power of healing by opening and allowing this inner force to flow. Give it time, space, and energy, and intentionally direct it to where it is needed most.

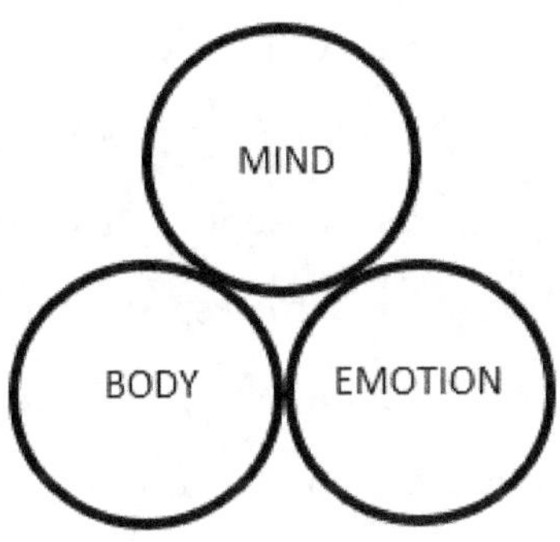

CHAPTER 2

TOOLS

As you are developing your powers, you will see that you have three main tools with which to use them. These tools are the mind, the body, and the emotions. This book identifies five primary functions of each tool which you will want to learn, practice, and master. The mind, body, and emotions are powerful tools that demand respect and development.

In our culture, respect is given to those who use the

mind, body, and emotions successfully and those who do not are shunned. This is a backward response because people are expected to know how to use their tools even though they haven't been taught. Thus, those with advantages and support have a head start on success. We must learn to respect and hold in high esteem the powers and tools we have. Self-respect enables the individual to care for and honor all that they are, all that they will become, and the path they take for self-development.

The mind, body, and emotions are described as tools because they are the very instruments through which we use our powers. Many people try not to think about or feel things because they don't understand or are afraid of the information or experience. We often learn to avoid what is uncomfortable instead of learning what is needed to feel comfortable and confident. So, people don't see the mind, body, and emotions as tools they can learn to use and, instead, get frustrated with and ignore them. Just like any tool we use, the mind, body, and emotions need to be taken care of, or they can be lost or damaged.

The mind is your tool for making decisions, for understanding, for interpreting and developing your world. It is already equipped with the ability to learn, problem-solve and experiment. It is the tool we use to direct our experiences, create, and determine the steps to accomplish goals. When we don't learn to use this tool, the mind is sloppy, cluttered, distracted, overwhelmed, confused and so on. We have difficulty making decisions and often make choices that hurt or fail. Our thinking can get so distorted that we can't tell what is real or true. We then have a hard time taking care of ourselves or finding enjoyment and are prone to let the emotions be our decision maker.

The emotions are your tool for obtaining information about the world around you, for identifying what you need and what supports you, and they add depth and richness to experiences. They provide valuable information with which the mind needs to consider its options and choices. This tool operates through the nervous system in the body, sending signals to the brain. Thus, we usually feel emotions through aspects of the physical body. For instance, when feeling nervous, we often sweat or feel "butterflies" in the stomach. When feeling excited, we can feel a burst of energy and tingling.

Emotions are the least understood tool and because of this we often learn to block or project them. No matter how much we try to ignore them, they will continue to be re-experienced until the mind makes sense of the information. Emotions are powerful signals that work by really getting your attention. Negative emotions signal that something very important is lacking. Many people get stuck in the feeling instead of interpreting the message of the signal. If an emotion signals a need, you want to start looking for ways to take care of it yourself. Emotions are a mysterious sense. We can feel the emotions of others and are often easily confused between another person's feelings and our own. This is another reason why understanding how to use the emotion tool is so important.

The body is your tool for experiencing the material or physical world. It enables you to influence the world and bring ideas and feelings into physical form. The body is a magnificent vehicle that has its own set of senses for receiving and sending information. The body is the tool that gets the most attention because it is seen and felt. However, even with what we know about the body, many people still don't have a personal understanding of how to take care of their own and many mysteries continue to perplex the medical system. The body supplies the mind and the emotions with nutrients, energy, and protection. As a tool, it is often damaged and deeper reflection on it's amazing ability to heal itself will help increase respect for its power.

These tools must be taken care of, valued, respected, and protected. You must distinguish your tools from the tools of others, but you can learn a lot by observing how others use their tools. We must protect our tools so that we maintain control and direction of them, so they will not be damaged by interactions with the world, and so we can take the time to focus on using them effectively. Protecting our tools means we pay attention to what or who attempts to influence us.

Protecting our tools involves physically protecting our personal space. This space is identified as the distance from the body to just past the fingertips of your outstretched arms. Imagine that distance around your head, down and around the bottom of your feet like an egg-shaped bubble. Protect that space around you by filtering what you allow next to it. In general, it is acceptable to stand about 4 feet away from people you don't know. We tend to stand about two feet away from people we do know. Take time to sit in a safe space daily to take care of and tune-in to all three tools.

Know that you are both alone in your space and are a part of everything around you at the same time. You want to get comfortable and practiced in both of these experiences so you will be able to shift as needed. You want to master your tools for your own self-development and master using your tools in the world.

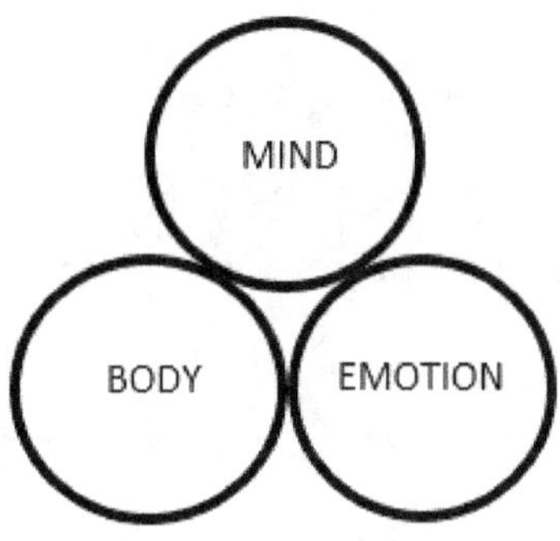

CHAPTER 3

FUNCTIONS

This book is about learning to develop and increase your powers by learning to use your tools effectively. There is so much to learn about being human that it takes a lifetime. Thus, it is wise to observe and learn from how others use their tools, but you still must practice to gain experience and master them. Each tool has several functions – ways that we use/operate them. For instance, a cell phone has many functions. We can use it to text, take photos, email, and play games.

The functions of the mind, body, and emotions allow you to explore the world, define and create what you want, discover, and develop yourself along the way. Learn to use all of the functions to determine the direction and purpose of your path, create meaning, and fully enjoy all aspects of your unique life.

The idea is to take direction of your tools as soon as you can so you can choose an enjoyable and fulfilling life - no matter what challenges, difficulties, or negative experiences you've had so far. Know that everyone comes into this world with different levels and capabilities of using the functions, so don't get off track by comparing yourself to others.

<u>Functions of the MIND</u>
<u>Thoughts</u>
Thoughts are where we process information. We will have both random thoughts that come from outside ourselves, some that are influenced or pushed on us by others and those that are our own and that we direct. Thoughts are information and you will want to filter through and determine what thoughts to keep and

what to clean up or throw out. If a negative thought keeps repeating, write it down and think about what message it is giving you. Learn to stop thoughts that don't support you and create habits of thought that encourage you. Thoughts can be fleeting so write them down so you can think more about it later. Take time to think about things and pay attention to what thoughts are in your mind in each moment.

Beliefs

Beliefs are habits of thought that are usually created from repeated experiences or what we've been taught by others. Beliefs are determined and solidified by the thoughts we choose to keep and those we agree with. They are useful in guiding our choices in the moment when we don't have time to think through. Beliefs function as a placeholder for understanding a subject, and we use them for many things including how we define ourselves, the world, and the lifestyle we choose.

If I don't feel good about a belief I am holding such that it creates fear or hurt, that belief is not helping me. I will want to get more information to further examine my belief and consider adjusting or changing it. This allows me to build on my understanding of life over a span of time and experiences. Expect to change your beliefs as you learn and grow and make sure they are working for you.

If I am conflicted about what I believe, I will have difficulty moving forward and making choices. Working with and changing beliefs is a process and takes time, intention, and patience. More experience with this will help you to also have more patience and understanding with others who have different beliefs.

Identity

Identity is a specific and very important belief that functions to define who I am and what I am doing. Identity allows us to hold our space on the planet and gives us reason to use our tools. It functions to take stock of what we have developed within the Self to this point. Before we learn to use this function, others offer feedback that influences the creation of our identity early on. However, you must take direction of this function of the mind as soon as possible because no one else can determine it for you.

Start by determining who you are right now. What are your interests, values, talents, strengths, weaknesses? What are you drawn to? When you look out at the world, what things do you like most? What things do you think about? What role do you usually take? For instance, I am a self-sufficient gardener, an artist, craft person, inventor, healer, weaver, counselor, mom. I love snow, trees, wild animals, birds, and all of nature. I like to learn from other cultures, dance, play games, and make movies. I can keep listing things.

You see, the point is to grow and expand who you are and what you do. My identity is defined by what I do. When I did not know who I was I felt lost and sad. Pick one thing that you "identify" with and start doing it a lot. Keep at it and it becomes a part of who you are. Even if you stop doing something for a long while, it is still part of who you are because you did it. We will identify with our mistakes until we correct them. The identity can be built and changed or grow - so have fun with it!

<u>World view</u>

World view is another specific and very important belief that functions to define our understanding and choices. It is usually based on what we have experienced in the world up to this point. As with any belief, your world view allows you to make choices without thinking through in the moment.

What we think and feel about the world is important for determining how to interact with it and how to utilize our tools. Remember, your world view will change throughout your life, but the important thing is that you know what your world view is at any given time. It is natural to feel uncertain about this view but any questions or concerns you have will help you form it. For instance, I worry that deforestation depletes wildlife habitat, and the removal of old growth trees increases glacial melt and global temperatures. Also, I just love forests, so I choose the view that forests should be protected. As a result, I have a forest of my own to protect and provide wildlife habitat. So, my world view guides my behavior and choices.

<u>Creativity</u>

Creativity is a function of the mind in which we receive or pull information in the form of ideas from seemingly higher intelligence. Its function is to create new forms or experiences and find solutions. When this function is blocked it can be hard to make decisions. To improve or activate this creativity you want to relax, open the mind to possibilities and set time aside to get it flowing. You want to have a positive attitude and trust that you can access creativity because we often have this function blocked and it can feel like a struggle. So don't fight it, rather relax, and open up.

Creativity is much like accessing the imagination where you let yourself play with ideas and have fun. You can use the imagination to start with an idea and then the mind begins to think of how to create it. This is when you know your creativity is flowing because you are actively taking steps to bring it into form. It is important to dedicate time each day to keep this function of the mind active as our world has many distractions and limitations that will easily deter you.

Functions of the EMOTIONS

Signals

Emotions function as signals of information through the nervous system. They signal whether an interaction or experience is positive or negative and therefore affects both the mind and the body. Because these signals travel quickly through the nervous system, are readily and often intensely felt in the body, take all the time you need to learn what the signals mean. As children, we often feel and respond immediately with a sort of knee-jerk reaction. We may project the emotion back onto others, run away, or freeze.

Strong signals can override the mind momentarily, so it is hard in the moment to think through what just happened. Strong signals indicate that the message behind it is of great importance. Such an important message requires the mind to process through. We must learn to step back from the situation and take the time to understand what message is being signaled before we make a choice of what to do next. Weaker signals are important too and are not to be ignored. They will nag you like a dull ache to get your attention.

Negative emotions signal that something is dangerous, wounded, harmful, or needed. Positive emotions signal balance, connection, support, or clarity. Because children have not yet learned that emotions act as signals and therefore react (most people don't think of them this way), other people will try to get them (or you) to stop responding or overreact to them also.

A sort of chain reaction can occur. Thus, some people learn, instead, to block emotional signals or hold them inside without ever understanding what its message is. Others may continue to project or reflect emotions back onto others, still not understanding the meaning but acting in a defensive manner. So, many adults never learn that emotions function as signals with meaning either. The emotional signals you get are yours and they will continue to signal you until you get the meaning. We can feel the emotions of others, so we must also be able to determine whether the signals are ours or theirs.

<u>Independence</u>
Emotions give us important information, but from the moment of birth, we also use them to communicate. It

is natural for us to let them override the mind and to have difficulty distinguishing our own from others'. We must learn as we grow how to understand, relate, and respond intentionally to our own emotional signals. Thus, another function of emotions is to establish the individual as an independent person.

Infants and children depend on the emotional signals from others to get what they need. They are vulnerable to the emotional intelligence of their parents or caregivers. If a parent has not learned emotional independence, they are not able to teach it to their child. In fact, they will often seek emotional reassurance from the child as they continue to do so from others. The child, of course, is not able to give reassurance that they need themselves so as a result there can be confusion and pain in family relationships.

You have learned to get around and take care of some basic needs independently, and now it is time to work with and use your tool of emotions independently. Begin to determine whether an emotion is yours or someone else's. Identify your emotional signal by name, take time to look for and understand the message, then take care of the wound or need, or acknowledge it as part of your identity if it is positive.

Spend time owning your emotions and let others deal with theirs. Don't get caught up in trying to understand another's emotions. Only you can best understand and take care of your emotions, so recognize when you are stuck in wanting someone else to respond in a specific way. This does not mean you shouldn't show care. You can acknowledge someone is upset, for instance, and briefly encourage them in finding a solution.

If I don't know what I am feeling, how is anyone else going to know? Even if they do have an idea, they will not be able to take care of it for me whenever I need it. So, as we learn to take care of our emotions alone, we become independent individuals and relieve others of the burden to take care of what they cannot. Emotional independence allows us to enjoy others without needing anything from them. This creates a great sense of stability within that we need to direct our life.

Self-love

Self-love is a function that enables an individual's emotions to stay open and connected. Love is an emotional signal on its own, but it also operates as a sort of conduit for life to flow through us. When we feel love for ourselves, we feel a flow of love within that comes from life itself. I first discovered this when I did not have self-love but realized that I was still able to give love to others. How can I give love to others, I thought, if I don't feel it myself? I realized that love always flows within us, but we cut it off or block it when we've experienced hurt or betrayal. So, because we've blocked the flow, we don't feel it and, in fact, it turns to self-hate. It is still there even though we try to close it off - usually as a means to protect ourselves.

When self-love is diminished in some way, we disconnect from feelings, both positive and negative, and then are not able to read, interpret and respond to the signals accurately. Self-love allows for the free flow of information that is important for growth and development. Love flows within because it is life itself. When we heal the emotional wounds or address the fears that caused us to block self-love, we open to learning from our negative emotions and gain a strong desire to increase experience of positive emotions.

To open the flow of love within, you must actively be kind, gentle, and encouraging to yourself. Love is life and life is the force that continually moves us to grow. Love is the most powerful healing force and is already flowing through you! As you open your emotions and let yourself feel, let the love flow to that part of you that is wounded or fearful. In the same way that you can give love to another through your outstretched hand, you can bring your hand to your heart and heal the wound that is blocking self-love. This is a process, meaning it doesn't happen after one time. You must repeatedly open to feeling self-love and work to expand it within. As you do, you begin to connect more with your life and your sense of Self.

Relationships

Relationships function to expand experiences and increase the signals we get from emotions. They can have a doubling effect. If a relationship feels good, there is resonance, and we feel the connection with others outside of ourselves as a doubling of positive emotion. If a relationship feels bad there is discord, and the negative emotion is doubled in intensity. Because the intensity of emotional signals is increased, we are often thrown way off track when it is negative.

This is why you want to learn to love and connect with yourself first, so you will know what to look for in a partner, friend, or group. Many people seek relationships to fill a part of themselves that seems to be missing. They may be drawn to someone who has a strength where they are weak. This can work out but continues to keep the individuals dependent on each other. Sometimes people seek relationships because they don't like to be alone or need someone to validate them, but this is something that people can never truly do for us. Our emotional needs cannot be fulfilled by another and continuing to expect it leaves one needy for attention.

The key is to find common ground with people and understand there are different levels of relationships.

The more we have in common with someone, especially regarding things that are important to us, the closer and deeper the relationship can become. This is where expansion of experience occurs. Learn to be okay with the fact that some relationships will remain superficial or just friendly in passing. When trying to connect with someone, determine the level that is best. You won't connect with everyone, deep connections are rare, and they often have to be sought after through trial and error. It is important to not try to force or coerce relationships. After several attempts, it is usually best to determine whether a person will remain at a lower level of connection or not at all. Remember the doubling effect. Learn to use your emotions to give you information about how to relate to others.

<u>Respect</u>

Respect is a vital function of emotions that is used to protect and value the Self. It is also a feeling that has a function or action. Respect must be activated for self-development to occur and can be defined as a level of self-development. Respect provides protection from outside influences which is needed so an individual can take the time needed to interpret all available information. To respect yourself you ensure your personal space is safe and nurturing. Only allow valuable influences to remain in your room or home.

To use respect as protection you may need to remove yourself from or avoid harmful interactions. Respect cannot be demanded from others; you must always respect yourself first. Once functioning effectively, respect can be given to others so that we honor their personal space. Depending on the person, they may or may not understand this as an act of respect, so it is important to state the intention clearly and avoid getting into an argument by politely removing yourself.

Respect is also used to value yourself, someone, or something. This is done by verbally acknowledging the aspects of value observed and appreciated. You build respect and therefore value by doing this consistently. Make a list and reflect on it often. Respect feels good and is absolutely necessary in life. Without it, wonton destruction, violence, neglect, hate, abuse, and the like, persist. We have become a world focused on demanding respect instead of giving it. If I have been devalued by another, I must know that I cannot force them to respect me, as they have already shown a lack of understanding of the function of respect.

If I continue to engage with them, I only further disrespect myself. Think of the doubling effect explained in the relationship section. If I continue to participate, I am only adding to the systemic problem. We must create a community of respect by actively participating with others in using this function of emotions. When I focus on building my value and recognize the value of others, the world is a better place.

Functions of the BODY

Energy

Energy is a function that enables all the body organs and systems including the mind and emotions to work effectively. The energy in our bodies is chemical, electrical, and light energy. We are constantly using and converting energy though we don't usually notice it unless we have a lot or too little energy. It is common knowledge that we get energy from food, but it is less common to know how different foods affect our energy. Many of the things that affect a person's energy level are still a mystery to the modern medical system.

Energy is utilized in all that we do, and it takes more energy to intentionally influence the world. There are many well-known body movements including yoga and Tai Chi that enable us to tune-in to, direct, and increase our flow of energy. These movements have been known for millennia to improve health, well-being, clarity, insight, and peace. To increase the flow of energy needed for big projects or feats, one needs to focus and use their energy consistently. As we use it, we draw more in and/or increase how much we use.

Children do a lot of growing physically so their bodies are pulling in a lot of energy – it's not just about how much they eat. As a result, children are also very active and don't realize they need rest until they stop moving for a moment. For another example, when someone is focused on something intently, their energy level will rise as they get inspired, excited, or even angry.

Begin to pay attention to your energy level throughout each day. If you have excess energy, what can you focus it into that is productive and helpful? Anxiety and stress energy are calling you to hone and channel your focus on a specific task or issue. Make sure to use the excess energy to help or improve, not cause damage or accidents. You may need to rest if your energy is low, but if you aren't able to, get your body moving or focus on something *until* your energy increases. This is why exercise is so important. Knowing that the longer you focus on something, the more energy will be drawn, will help you to keep at it till it begins to flow without effort. Seek information to understand what energy is both within us and that which we use every day to power our machines.

Grounding

Grounding functions to bring the mind's focus to the body, increase ability to be present in the moment and to release excess electrical energy from the body. Grounding is the movement of our own energy down into the earth. While this is largely done through the force of gravity already, we need to understand and use this function so that we stay focused in our bodies. Humans use the mind in more ways than other creatures, such that sometimes our focus can get stuck in thoughts. This can cause problems when a person is not paying attention to what is going on with and around them. They may be thinking of the past, the future, or worries and concerns. This puts one off balance and grounding is needed.

Grounding is done through the legs via various movements including walking and squats. Grounding helps one to develop a strong physical presence and to maintain inner and outer balance. Whenever you have excess energy that you are unable to channel through a specific focus, grounding is necessary to disperse the build up electrical energy in the nervous system.

<u>Breathing</u>

Breathing occurs naturally of course but when understood as a function of the body, it can be utilized intentionally to calm the nervous system, clear, and focus the mind, and replenish energy. None of the automatic systems of the body should be taken for granted and ignored, least of all the breath. We cannot exist without it. We take in oxygen and the cells break it down, converting it to chemical energy. So, the more oxygen you take in the more energy is available to the cells.

Ancient cultures and their spiritual beliefs and practices have long understood the power of intentional breathing. Many meditation practices instruct the individual to keep the body still while focusing on the breath. This allows all the energy taken in to be used for regeneration, healing, and balancing rather than work. Taking breaks in your day to focus on breathing helps keep your energy flowing and therefore all your systems run smoothly and efficiently. With your focus channeled on your breath, the mind is also allowed to rest. This helps to slow the mind and clear it of scattered activity.

There are many breathing techniques out there so trying several and finding out what works for you is the key. Start off small. You can work on stopping to breathe before a stressful situation or conversation and breathing through it. Take a long breath just before starting a task and notice how it helps you focus. The mind requires a lot of energy to work effectively so providing it with a boost and continuous supply throughout a task will do wonders.

Relaxation

Relaxation is a necessary function of the body to open all the system pathways, allowing things to flow with ease. Constriction of air flow, circulation, or energy negatively affects the body but also the mind and emotions. Relaxation can be used to tune-in to the body and increase your awareness of what is being constricted. Pain or discomfort in the muscles, organs or tissues usually indicate blockage or damage. Relaxing is important for taking the time to identify a problem early on when it is easier to attend to.

When you relax a disturbed area on purpose, you help to open the body's circulation which allows cells that detoxify and heal to move in. If you are feeling stress or excitement, that tension can cause constriction. So, use relaxation consistently and often for healing and specifically during stressful situations to increase awareness and focus. Learn to practice relaxing your muscle groups by simply focusing and dropping areas one at a time. The more you practice, the more deeply you will be able to relax and be able to maintain an ongoing relaxed state. Again, ancient cultural practices that teach relaxation have been known and practiced for millennia. It takes time to practice, and it is about tuning-in to feeling the subtleties of your body. It also feels really good to be deeply relaxed and yet awake and focused at the same time.

<u>Sleep</u>

Sleep is a function of the body that allows for repair, rest, and resetting systems. It is a deeper state of relaxation that is necessary for optimal functioning. We need a safe space without disruptions to ensure that we are able to let go of the conscious wake state and descend into the subconscious state. There are four stages of sleep that cycle many times during several hours of sleep. Your subconscious is an important part of you. It is very active during sleep but is not outside your influence and direction.

To improve sleep, take care of any physical needs and then lay in a sleep position that enables you to relax and close your eyes. Command your subconscious to have a deep and rejuvenating sleep. Plan to address any other concerns you may have during your wake state so that your sleep will not be disturbed. If there are time constraints or you are tired during the day be sure to give yourself 10 to 15 minutes for a nap using the same instructions. This will allow you to reset and you can catch up on your sleep cycle later.

The mind is very active during most of the sleep cycles. It is processing information, and the imagination has free range. Sometimes it will get our attention and wake us up providing solutions, ideas, or highlighting fears and worries. Use this information if you can to move forward in a positive way with an issue but keep in my that the primary function of sleep is to repair and reset. Some people get caught up in the mysterious world of sleep such that they avoid focusing in the wake state. Some may be afraid to sleep and don't get the rest that is necessary for effective functioning. Seek balance.

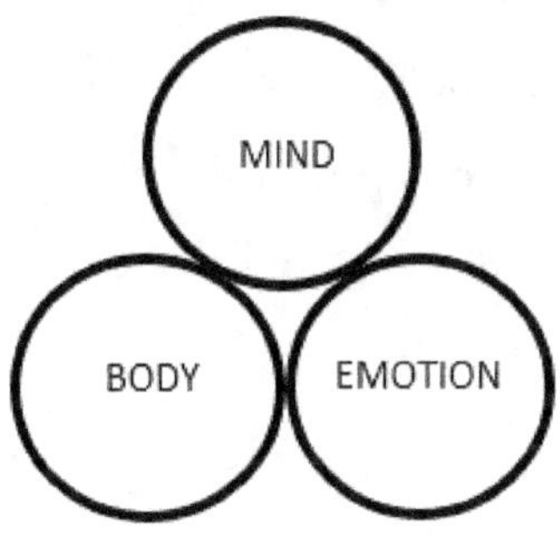

CHAPTER 4

SKILLS

Our powers and tools with all their various functions need to be intentionally practiced and used because life can be dangerous, complicated, fragile, confusing, and dysfunctional without them. Hopefully, younger generations will learn to master them sooner so the lifestyles and experiences our communities choose to engage in support the health, well-being, joy, balance, and beauty of all living beings. Most people learn about their powers and tools but do not recognize them as such and are not using them intentionally. As a result, people frequently struggle with the following skills. This is because the skills incorporate the use of several powers and/or tools. So, if you don't understand and master the basics, you will have greater difficulty developing further.

Processing

Processing is a skill that involves awareness, reflecting, interpreting, and analyzing so at its core it is really problem-solving. The word processing is chosen here, however, to emphasize the importance of looking at as much information as possible in order to more deeply understand a subject. The following steps are provided to clarify how to learn the skill. Learn to use all of the powers to process all the functions of mind, body, and emotions. We must be able to process thoughts, feelings, and behaviors every moment of every day to make choices that support and create well-being.

Processing steps

1)Awareness. Be aware of the thoughts, feelings, and behaviors you are engaging in all throughout the day.

Pay attention when the signals are active. It is easy to get caught up in an event or situation such that you don't even notice the strong signals your nervous system is sending you. The less we notice or avoid, the more we become desensitized to signals. We must be aware of them, stop what we are doing, and process the signal.

2)Observe details. Stop what you are doing and tune-in to the details. What are the details and the message of this thought, feeling or behavior? What is going on? Look at the experience through your senses and let yourself fully observe the information coming to you. Take at least 10 minutes to go through the details.

3)Determine the need. A negative thought, feeling or behavior signals that something is lacking. Remember that you can only interpret the meaning for yourself accurately, not for another. If the actions of another created the signal, you still need to ask what *you* need. The need is usually the opposite of the negative thought, emotion, or behavior. Take a little time to reflect and think through this. What is lacking? What do you need that you don't currently possess? Identify the opposite of what you are feeling, thinking or doing.

4)Determine a response. When you have identified what you need you will now want to identify how to address and attend to this need for yourself. This may mean you need to change a repeating negative thought to one that is more supportive. If there is an emotional need you will want to pick something that will help you to feel the needed positive emotion. If it is a behavior, you will want to determine a new behavior to replace the negative one or the one that didn't obtain the desired outcome. Follow through on the new response now. Write it down, memorize it, and practice it daily.

5)Recognize the shift. Each time you replace the old response with the new response take a moment to notice what about that experience shifted. Did the new thought support you and feel better? Did the new action produce the desired positive emotion even just a little? Was the new behavior more effective or successful in obtaining the desired outcome?

Once you process through an issue you will now need to put the new decision into practice and make the change to the new habit. Make sure you take the time to process fully before you begin. Now focus on awareness by catching yourself in the old habit, replacing it with the new response, and recognizing the shift. Continue to do this as best you can every day for around 30 days. This will create a new habit of response. Recognize fully that *you* did it!

Letting go

Sometimes we get caught up in an issue and just get stuck. I can't move forward no matter how hard I try; I can't find a resolution and the issue is still at the forefront of my mind. This is often something we have spent a good amount of time thinking about and trying to work on. Now we must let go of finding a resolution. I must use all my powers of awareness, choice, focus, habit, value, balance, and healing.

Letting go is a practice of thought stopping and directing focus. It will likely prompt the eventual changing of a belief (identity or worldview) and/or activate respect and independence. We have to choose, every time the thoughts come up, to stop thinking about the issue in any way. It may be a feeling you need to let go of. You will have to choose to not let yourself continue to feel the feeling. In order to stop thoughts and feelings, we have to choose to direct our focus on something else (as suggested above) repeatedly until the urge to think or feel the issue subsides.

This can take several days to accomplish depending on how strongly the issue has affected you, but it is well worth it. Once you finally let go, you will feel relief and freedom, and you will also be open to new ideas. When we are stuck and closed off, we can't access new information, look from new perspectives, and block healing. Resolution to the original problem may come after you finally let go, but if not, you will be free to move in an entirely new direction. Focus and direct the functions of the mind and emotions to move ahead.

Trust

Trust is a skill that applies the power of awareness and choice, the skill of processing, and utilizes the functions of the mind (beliefs and thoughts), emotions (relationships and respect), and likely grounding. Trust must be chosen based on experience not just freely given. Trust is based on the consistent observation of facts that are beneficial and witnessed over a long period of time.

Based on these facts, an individual will still have to choose to trust. When trust is lost, it will take a long period of observed behaviors to regain it. Fear of trusting others can come up and grounding and respect will need to be utilized. Developing this skill will help you gain or regain peace in life. When you know who and what you trust in, the world feels like a safer place.

First you want to learn to trust yourself and the same rules apply. If this is difficult, address the issue by processing to determine what is needed, and use the power of healing to help you take the time to open up. Then, consistently follow through and, over a long enough period - perhaps a year, - you can reasonably choose to trust your ability in that area. If you don't trust in yourself first, it will be difficult to trust others.

Communication

Communication is a skill that enables a good flow of information. It is a process that may require the use of the powers of awareness, choice, values, balance, and healing. The functions of relationship, respect, beliefs, identity, creativity, independence, energy, and relaxation will likely also need to be activated.

Communication involves listening, the skill of processing, and uses respect to express resonance and understanding. Writing in a reflection and processing journal is a way of communicating with yourself and is very helpful when you need to express your thoughts and feelings but know others may conflict with or misunderstand you. When others are involved, it is best to decide to communicate after the processing has turned to understanding. You may need to get more information from the other person so you can process your own thoughts and feelings and consider theirs.

You may need time to reach some understanding and more to clarify how to express it so another will be more apt to listen. Give yourself time in the whole process. When you don't understand, let the other know that you will think about it and get back to them. Also leave yourself room to request more information if needed. If you don't take the time to understand and clarify your own views, it will be difficult to consider another's or communicate clearly and effectively. To further develop this skill, learn to use words to access and project the power of healing.

Collaboration

We have been taught that competition is a good way for people to excel, so collaboration is not a well-developed or common skill. Collaboration is when people work together to achieve a goal. If you can see communication as a collaboration, you may find it easier to go through the process. When you know what your strengths are and you value the strengths of others, you can find ways to combine them to achieve something greater than what one could do alone. So, to collaborate you will likely use most if not all the powers, several functions including relationships, respect, energy, independence, creativity, and skills like processing, trust, and communication.

Collaboration focuses on individuals identifying and utilizing their strengths, enables the development of personal values, and creates a supportive community. Utilize respect, trust, belief, choice, relationship, and identity at the very least to successfully collaborate. Join a team or group to learn and practice this skill.

Many groups may still value some individuals more than others. A true collaboration will clearly identify, actively value, and honor each member's contribution and level of control, provide autonomy, and utilize their creativity. A leader may be needed to determine the parameters and direction of the project or business, but everyone involved is publicly recognized as a vital collaborator and treated with upmost respect. This allows communication to flow and enables greater ease during adjustments and growth.

Several very successful companies were made from collaborations. We create health, happiness, and unique beauty when we work together and support each other's growth. Value begins within the individual then extends to the family, group, and the planet. Your self-development and collaboration **will** make the world a better place and may be the key to healing cultural, religious, generational, and environmental traumas that continue to divide us.

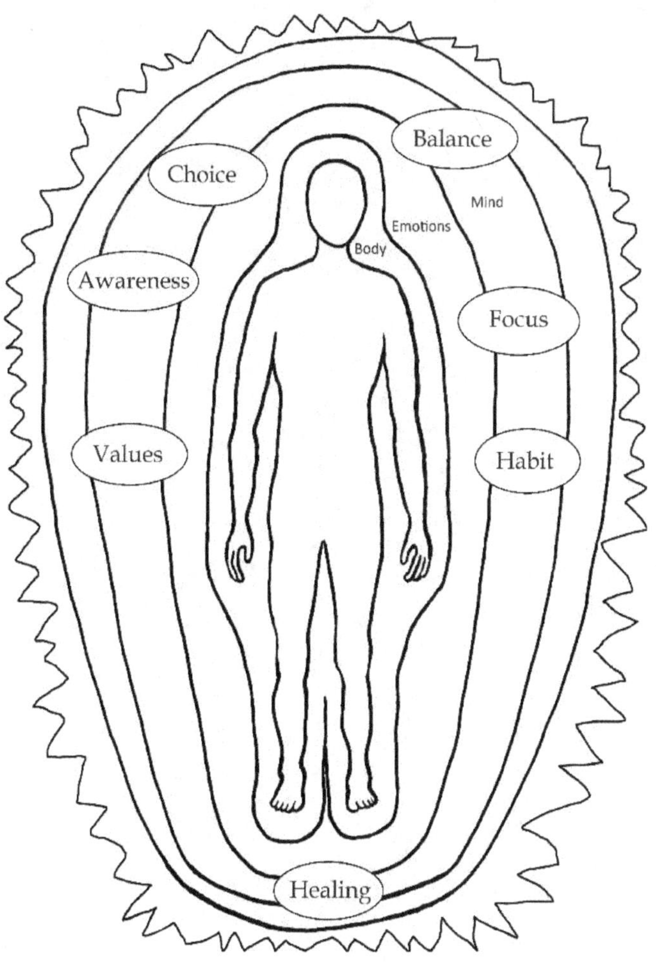

These are your great powers and tools.
Use them intentionally to develop yourself,
and create a fulfilling life.

ABOUT THE AUTHOR

Judy Moore has worked in the mental health field for ten years as a counselor and crisis interventionist utilizing cognitive behavioral therapy among other interventions. This book is a culmination of the concepts and techniques she utilized, adapted, and created to help clients understand and direct the mind, body, and emotions more effectively.

Judy earned a Bachelor of Science in Psychology from Fayetteville University, a Master of Public Administration from Brandman University, and began exploring and studying energy work through reflexology and Reiki in the late 1990's. She earned a Reiki Master Certification in 2021.

Judy lives with her husband in Washington and has four wonderful children. She is an artist, gardener, herbalist, and weaver with a great love of the natural world.

9 798985 188639